The Great Tooth Chase

Printed in the United States of America

ISBN: 13:978:1512036893

Turtleback Publishing

To my good friends who love both kids and dogs (though not necessarily in that order) and who live their own wild adventures -- Charlotte Brothers and Linda Burket.

The Great Tooth Chase

By CB Simmons

Table Of Contents

Chapter 1

"No. It'll hurt." Lisa clamped her small hand across her mouth and pushed herself back against the wall by her bed.

"Sweetheart, just let me take a look," I begged my 6-year-old daughter once more to allow me to examine her loose front tooth.

"No Daddy. I don't want to pull it."

"Lisa, it has to come out. It might loosen during the night. You could swallow it in your sleep. Now open up." She looked up at me with wide eyes, shocked at the idea of swallowing that tiny nub of tooth wobbling now in her mouth.

"I hate teeth. Why do I have to lose them anyhow?"

"It's just the way of it. The baby teeth have to make room for your permanents. I started losing my baby teeth too when I was your age. Besides, the Tooth Fairy pays pretty well for teeth these days. I got only ten cents for my teeth under the pillow. Just last week your brother got four quarters for one of his molars. You could use that money in your piggy bank, couldn't you?"

"No. I'd rather just keep the teeth I have. I don't need permamumts." Her small arms folded decisively across her chest.

I dropped beside her on the bed. "You know, your tooth troubles make me think me of your great-grandfather."

"Do you mean Poppy? How come, Daddy?"

*Lisa's interest suddenly shifted to my words. She
loved the stories I told about my grandfather.*

*"He wanted to keep his teeth too, and one
time he lost them in a very strange way." I reached
over and pulled Lisa onto my lap. "Let me tell you . . . .*

"I'll be home around four-thirty Andy," she
announced. "Enjoy the candy. And, stop
scratching."

The door closed behind my mother and I
mimicked her words. "Stop scratching, stop
scratching. Is that all anybody can say?" Still holding
the bag of candy, I leaned against the doorjamb and
rubbed my tingling back hard against the

woodwork, like a bear against a woods pine. Just like that bear, I grunted in delight. That felt soooo good! Chicken Pox had kept me home from school for over a week, and I was bored! Besides, the itching was about to drive me bonkers. My skin was positively pink with Calamine lotion, and the little tufts of white cotton balls were stuck in the smears of dried medicine. Poppy said I looked like a used wad of cotton candy.

My family tried hard to keep me and my scratching hands busy. Poppy, my grandfather, entertained me with a running game of Monopoly set up at the dining room table. Mom would drop off little surprises over her lunch hour – a video game, a book from my school reading list, and just

now a small green-striped bag from the Super
Scooper Candy Shop.

We three always helped each other out that
way, like families are supposed to do. There were
just us three since my Grandma Betty had died. My
parents had split up right before my eighth
birthday, and my father was never around at all.
But, it didn't much matter anymore since he and I
never got along too well. We three liked being
together – Poppy, whose name was James Walker
Sloan, my mother, Claire Sloan-Tate, and me,
Andrew Walker Tate.

Poppy had shared our home for two years
now, moving in just a few weeks after my
grandmother's funeral. Just before she died,

Grandma Betty made my mother promise to help Poppy go on without her. I guess more than anything, Grandma Betty wanted him to remarry, and talked lots about it those last few days in the hospital. She insisted that it was Mom's job to help him find a new wife. Mom made the promise, and Grandma knew then that Poppy would be okay.

So Poppy came to live with us, bringing along his collection of CD's, a bookcase of history books, two dozen baseball caps, and his toothy grin, a smile that reminded us of one of those presidents whose faces are carved on that mountainside in North Dakota. His upper teeth, at least a few of them, were false, fixed to a partial plate. Poppy had lost his own teeth long ago. They'd been ripped out one wintry Saturday of Poppy's high school

sophomore year. He and some friends were firing

snowballs at one another. Poppy, running to escape

a volley of the cold, hard missiles, forgot to duck

under a neighbor's backyard clothesline, and the

wire caught him right across his mouth. He went

down hard! His buddies gathered around and

helped him get back home, Poppy carrying his

bloodied upper front teeth home in his hand. Over

the next few weeks Poppy's dentist fitted him with

a partial plate of bright white front teeth.

Poppy still wore that same partial plate. He

had taken very good care of it over the years and

was very proud of his smile. Even as a long-haul

trucker, he had worn out plenty of toothbrushes

just to keep his teeth pearly white. Everybody knew James Walker Sloan by his smile. His favorite joke was "My teeth are like stars. They come out at night."

His stacks and stacks of books were important too, almost as much as his smile. He loved to read and to spent lots of time with his book-loving buddies at the 8th Avenue Senior Center, the local hang-out for anybody in town who was really old and not working a regular job.

But our family was the most important thing to Poppy. He called us the Three Musketeers. Mom said we were more like the Three Stooges. She never liked the Musketeers too much. Poppy would just flash a toothy grin and ask if it was really better to be like three bumbling goofs who poked each other in the eye. Anyhow, whether Musketeers or Stooges, both groups stuck together through all kinds of adventures, just like my Mom, my Grandpa, and me.

And, the Sloan-Tate household had plenty of adventures. Sometimes even visiting the bathroom was as wild as the water canyon ride of a theme park. The toilet had a mind of its own, Poppy claimed. Unless the handle was jiggled just right, that stupid toilet would overflow every time! The rushing water would surge across the room, turn the bath mat into a floating island, and dump over the wastebasket, spilling trash everywhere. We would call out to one another, "Jiggle the handle," as a reminder to avoid soaking the floor and ourselves in

the backwash. Maybe we should have been calling

out, "Surf's up!"

Chapter 2

"I think I would have liked Poppy," Lisa's

brown eyes held my attention. "He sounds funny."

"Oh, he was, for sure." I stopped to remember

for a moment. "I miss him."

"Tell me more, Daddy," my daughter leaned

into me and waited for me to continue . . . .

Flopping down at the table where Poppy sat

at the Monopoly game, I opened the little bag while

my grandfather took his turn with the dice. Inside

the bag were all my favorite kinds of gum. I chose a

juicy-looking piece and tossed it into my mouth. .

"Your turn," Poppy said. I rolled the dice and moved

my battleship four spaces forward. "Ha! Vermont

Avenue. Pay up, bud," he held out a huge hand for my Mono money, as he called it.

"Okay, okay. I'm gonna' run out of money soon." Grabbing a handful of bills, I chomped noisily on my gum and blew a monstrous blob that popped loudly in my face.

"Ugh. That's disgusting." I offered the candy bag to him, but he waved it away. He didn't care for such elementary things, he said. Only children like bubble gum.

"That's alright, Poppy. You probably couldn't blow a bubble anyway," I mouthed the words around a pink blob that bounced against my lips.

"What's that mean?" Poppy asked absently.

His fingers rolled the dice across the table.

"Too old," I garbled around my gum. "It

takes lots of lung power to blow bubbles."

"You're scratching again. Stop it," he

warned. "And, whaddaya mean 'too old'?" Poppy's

chest swelled out, straining his shirt buttons. "I'll

show you old. Andrew, give me some of that gum." I

held the bag out to him, and he dug around inside it,

studying the options. There were brightly colored

goobers that smelled sweet and grapey, eyeballs

staring back unblinkingly from the bottom of the

bag, tear-jerkers so sour they could make a bully

cry, and fireballs that could set off a 3-alarm blaze

on your tongue. Poppy picked at the choices. He

held up an eyeball and winced in disgust, then fingered a fireball. But the warning look on my face told him to choose differently. He finally took a yellow goober. Tossing the gum into his mouth, my grandfather began to chew slowly.

"Kinda' hard. Just give me a minute to get this goo softened and ready to blow." He wallowed the ooze between his teeth and continued talking. "Why, back when I was your age, Andy, I blew huge bubbles, monster bubbles, bubbles the size of . . . "Poppy stopped in mid-sentence, his eyes wide in shock. Lifting his hand to his lips, he spit out the offending wad. Staring at the sticky yellow gob, Poppy groaned pitifully. "For cath thake – my teeth."

I tried hard to keep from laughing aloud at Poppy's strange speech while together we examined the slippery mound of goo lying in his hand. They were stuck there, both of Poppy's front teeth, broken off from his upper partial plate. Slapping his other hand over his mouth, Poppy roared out, "Look what you've done, boy. My thmile ith ruined!" Poppy abruptly disappeared into his room, grousing aloud as he went. From inside he called frantically, "Andy, what time ith your mother thuppothed to be home?"

"She said four-thirty, Poppy." I checked the kitchen clock. "It's four-ten now." I padded down the hall to his room in stocking feet. "Should I call her at the office?"

Before he could answer, the front door opened and Mom's voice called out, "Hey, you two. I'm home early for a change. How about a home-cooked meal tonight?"

I met her coming down the hallway. "You'd better get to Poppy's room. He needs you—bad." Mom dumped her purse into my arms and raced toward his room. He was pacing madly, speeding like a tennis ball across the net on a summer afternoon. His arms crossed his chest, fists folded, knuckles white.

"Pop, what's wrong?" He made no answer, but held up his open palm to her. There lay the two pearly-white teeth. Mom picked them from Poppy's hand, holding them up to the fading sunlight. Poppy whirled and made a fake smile at the mirror,

revealing a gaping hole where the teeth should have

been.

"Claire, I look like a thikth-year-old," he

lisped. "Good Grief, I thound like one too." More

pacing. "What am I gonna' do?"

Mom tried to comfort him. "Now Pop, it's

nothing that can't be fixed. How did this happen

anyway?" Poppy said nothing—just glanced in my

direction and dropped his head.

"The bubble gum you brought me at

lunchtime, "I began. "Poppy decided to show me

how he used to . . . "

Poppy's lisping words cut me off. "I wath

jutht acting a fool, Claire. Doing thomething I'm

really too old to do." Poppy then gave us both a real grin, toothless but real. "And, you can both thop hiding your laughter. I know I thound funny."

"Sure, Dad." Mom and I glanced at each other and giggled nervously. Poppy flopped onto the window seat. "What am I gonna' do?"

"Pop, I don't understand why you're so upset. It's simply a matter of taking the pieces down to Dr. Benton's office. A little dental glue and your teeth will be fine, good as new. I can run them by the dentist when I go to the grocery store."

Whipping around and charging at my mother, Poppy wailed, "But Claire, how long will it take?"

"How long? I don't know," she stammered.

"A day or two, maybe. Let's see, this is the eleventh.

You should have them back by the fourteenth,

Pop." Mom eyed him suspiciously. "Why the rush?"

"Are you thure, Claire? Are you thure I'll have

them back by Thaturday?" His words hurried out as

Poppy spit into the air with each S. I could see little

droplets fly past his lips and swan dive onto his shirt.

"The fourteenth is Valentineth Day, you know."

Poppy turned away and fingered the window

curtains.

"Yes, I remember that it's Valentines Day.

Why does that matter so much?"

"I've jutht got thomething to . . . it's jutht that I . . . oh Claire, " Poppy pivoted and plopped down on the bed.

Mom shrieked and nearly flew across the carpeted floor. Grabbing hold of her father, she led him in a two-step around the room, all the while singing out, "You're gonna' ask her, you're gonna' ask her."

"Here here. Not tho rough, young lady." Poppy protested mildly. He smiled then, an embarrassed show of gappy teeth, and skipped along with her. Mom finally dropped to the bed, smiling a huge face-breaking grin.

"Dad, I think it's wonderful!"

I watched their waltz curiously, wondering
what brought on such excitement from my mother.
Finally I thrust myself between them. "What's
wonderful?" They both faced me, then one another.

"Thould we tell him?" Poppy lisped out.

"Only if you want to tell, if you're ready."
Mom sat quietly now and waited on her father.

My grandfather reached out to pull me down
beside him. "Andy, do you remember Mith
Emerthon?"

"Mith Emerthon?" I repeated the garbled
words, then translated for myself. "O, Miss
Emerson. Of course I remember her, Poppy."

"Well, you know that thhe and I have been
keeping company lately."

Now I was thoroughly confused. "Huh? What does keeping company mean?"

"Dating," Mom interjected. "Go on, Dad."

My eyes widened. Dating? My grandfather . . . dating???

He continued. "We've been theeing eathh other for theveral weekth now." That I knew was so. Miss Emerson had been Poppy's main topic of conversation lately. I knew they were spending lots of time together over at the 8th Avenue Senior Center. Mom had even mentioned her often when she and I had kitchen duty together every evening.

"Well, thhe and I get along fine and . . . and, I'm going to pop the quethtion."

More confusion scurried around in my head. "Pop the question? What does . . . ?"

"To marry him," Mom's word burst out and bubbled into the air. "Your grandfather's getting married again, Andy." This time I became her unwilling dance partner and she waltzed me around Poppy's bed while I tried to make sense of what I had just heard.

"Married?" My mouth played with the word. "To Miss Emerson? Is that good?"

"Good? It's wonderful!" Mom was still dragging me through the dance when she saw Poppy's dejected face. "What's wrong?"

"Clarie, how can I propothe to Jane Ellen with two teeth miththing?" He moved to the mirror to examine his damaged smile.

Mom's face reflected behind Poppy's in the mirror. "Don't worry, Pop. I'll call Dr. Benton's office right away. He'll have those teeth back to you in two days, tops." Planting a kiss squarely on his cheek, Mom went in search of her purse and cell phone, humming *"Here Comes The Bride."*

For my part, I chose to disappear to my room. Despite Mom's obvious delight and Poppy's guarded happiness over Jane Ellen Emerson, I had a bad feeling. Our lives were about to change. Did I want that to happen?

Chapter 3

"Why did you have a bad feeling, Daddy?"
Lisa snuggled into my side, now more interested in my
story-telling than her wobbly tooth. "Didn't you like
Miss Emerson?"

"Yes, I did." I answered my daughter, smiling
down at her upturned little face. "But, there's a lot
more to this story."

"Goodie, I love long stories. Tell me. And, be
sure to talk more like Poppy when his teeth were
missing. It sure sounds funny!"

Mom carried the broken partial parts off to
the dentist's office right away and was told that
repairs would certainly be made by the fourteenth,

Valentine's Day. She returned home, then spent the evening on the phone with real estate calls, and Poppy disappeared into his room. I soon heard twanging guitar chords of a country song, and knew that Poppy was lost in listening to his favorite CD's. He would also be scanning the pages of Miss Emerson's latest loaner book, something on the Mexican Mayan temple ruins. She was always loaning another book to my grandfather.

That left me alone for the evening with plenty of thinking time. And, I discovered I was forced to think about Jane Ellen Emerson, the funny lady who buzzed around town in her little blue car, with boxes of books neatly stacked in the back. I recalled then that Mom had mentioned her often in the last few weeks. I should have guessed that something was up.

Kids all over town knew her as Miss Jane. She was a very important part of our lives as the story reader in the children's department of our local library. In character as "The Book Granny," she wore silly hats and carried a magic 'wand', actually an oversized wooden spoon. She had a wardrobe of brightly colored aprons with huge pockets made of hot pad holders. Those pockets always carried bite-size, cellophane-wrapped cookies that Miss Jane would hand out to her young listeners when story time ended. Sometimes she told the story using a hand puppet, and she always did funny voices of the book characters as she faithfully read to us every

Saturday morning. I remember sitting on the floor by that old white rocking chair while Miss Jane read of singing dinosaurs, mice who danced, pigs who flew space ships to faraway places. Saturday Story Time was always a great treat for us because of Miss Jane.I finally outgrew Story Time, but not before that gray-haired grandma had turned me into a marathon reader.

Miss Emerson and Poppy first met at the 8th Avenue Senior center. One evening the retired librarian gave a book review on one of Poppy's favorite subjects, travels through Mexico. When she finished, Poppy introduced himself and offered coffee and a piece of pie at Smarts' Café. He claimed he wanted to hear more about the Mayan

Indians of Mexico. Soon they were spending time together, mostly over books and coffee. Then they joined a "Walk For Exercise" group at the local YMCA, and a few weeks later it was dinner and a movie.

Mom told me all kinds of things about Poppy and Miss Jane while we washed the dinner dishes that evening. According to Mom, Poppy thought of Miss Jane as a good listener. He said he could be himself with her. When they first met and started spending time together, he talked to her about Grandma Betty, and Miss Jane listened and was sad with him. Then, I guess one day Poppy finished talking about Grandma Betty and knew that he wanted to listen to Miss Jane for a change. He spent more and more time with the library story lady.

Poppy had fallen in love, and my mother couldn't

have been happier about it.

But, not everybody in the Sloan-Tate house

was happy about it. I wasn't ready to share Poppy. I

didn't figure there was room for a fourth Musketeer.

Chapter 4

"Musketeer?" Lisa frowned in thought. "Isn't that the name of a candy bar?" She nodded hopefully. "Do we have any of those in the kitchen?"

I chuckled at her. "No, we don't. And, the Three Musketeers were soldiers, guards in the royal courts of France."

"What's that?"

"I'll tell you about that another time. Where are your PJ's? It's nearly your bedtime, Sweetie"

"Oh please, tell me more about Poppy and Miss Jane, Daddy. I'm nowhere near ready to go to sleep yet." Lisa stifled a yawn and looked up at me earnestly.

"Tell you what, get out your PJ's, and I'll tell you more while you get ready for bed."

My young daughter smiled slyly then, "Daddy, should you go to the kitchen first?"

I gave her a confused look. "Why would I do that?"

"You're not wearing an apron like Miss Jane did. Mommy has a bright red one out there. . . it's got great big, ugly flowers on it," her giggle infected me too, and I pulled Lisa into my arms.

"Alright, you, let's get back to the story. . . .

The next morning Mom announced I could return to school. The itches were gone, and I was glad to leave the house, but not really glad to be back in history class. I just didn't care about the battle of Gettysburg. Instead, a much more important battle was going on in my head – the awful thought of losing my wonderful grandfather to that busybody ex-librarian.

As hard as I tried, I couldn't get my brain to land on any other subject except Poppy. *"He can't leave! We need him. This feels too much like when Dad walked away from us. I hate it!"* History class was a nightmare and Math was no better. Mrs. Parker called on me to answer a math problem, but her voice didn't even register in my brain. She threatened to send me to the principal's office if I didn't pay better attention to the class. Then, I finally got a break – lunch followed by Gym class.

We were doing weight training, so I beat the snot out of the heavy bag in the weight room. I pretended it was wearing a silly hat and held a puppet on one hand.

School ended, and still my brain whirled, *"Poppy and I share summer baseball. Will he stop coaching if he marries Miss Emerson? Where will they live? For sure, not with Mom and me. Miss Emerson has a new double-wide at the Sunny Acres Home Park. Is there room in it for all Poppy's stuff?"* Teachers had yelled at me all day. I was go glad when that final afternoon bell rang, and was soon home, the front door closed behind me. Mom was there already, fixing dinner. She called out a cheery hello. I grunted, "Anything to eat? I'm starving."

Dropping my book bag on the kitchen table, I scrounged in the refrigerator for a snack. Then I did something really stupid.

The front door opened. It was Poppy, back from his usual afternoon walk with Miss Emerson, a book tucked under his arm. Eyes twinkling, he laid the book before me on the kitchen table. "Jane Ellen found thomething the thought would interetht you," he lisped.

I scanned the book's title -- "<u>Bubble</u> <u>Gum</u> <u>Glory</u> – <u>A</u> <u>History</u>." I heard Mom chuckle softly, but I didn't join her in Miss Emerson's little joke. Scooting my chair back, I pushed past Poppy toward my bedroom. "Tell her no thanks," I mumbled. "I have enough books to read already." I could feel Poppy's disappointment as his eyes followed me.

After dinner, while Mom and I washed dishes, she rattled on and on about Jane Ellen Emerson – how nice she was – how she really cared about Poppy – how bright and active in the community – how good she was for Poppy – how she encouraged activity for him. She would keep him young, Mom said. I let her go on for a while, trying to ignore the chatter, but I was soon sick of it. I didn't want to hear another word about Jane Ellen Emerson, the person who was taking my grandfather away from me. "I think they'll be great together," Mom commented cheerfully while handing me a freshly washed plate.

I finally mustered the words. "Could we talk about something else?"

Mom stopped, stunned. "What did you say?"

"I don't want to talk about Miss Emerson." I rubbed hard at a spot on the plate. I guess I was trying to rub that old librarian from my mind.

Mom's eye lingered on me. "Andy, why don't you want me to talk about Poppy and Jane Ellen?"

"You know why, Mom."

"Tell me what's bothering you, son." She faced me squarely, but I couldn't meet her eyes. I stared down at the plate in my hands and swallowed hard. "Mom, I'm not sure about Poppy's marrying Miss Emerson. She's not much like Grandma Betty. Will he really be happy with her?"

Mom said nothing. She waited. I continued to swipe at the now dry plate in my hand, feeling her eyes fixed on me. I stammered on, "What if she wants to leave here – move to some other town, or even to another country." My voice rose a notch. "You know how she likes to travel." That was true enough. Since retiring, Miss Emerson had cruised the Caribbean, flown to Cancun, Mexico, traveled to Ireland, taken three bus tours across the country, and visited her friends in Toronto. "What if she finds another place that she really likes and talks Poppy into moving?"

Mom took hold of my wrists, me gripping the plate between us. "Andy, you won't lose him.

This isn't like the situation with your father. Poppy is not walking out on us."

My angry words sprang out, "Yes, he is. He's going away from us. To be with HER!"

Mom lowered her voice, "Son, I repeat that Poppy is not your father."

"But, that's what Dad did, Mom. He chose to leave us, leave me, leave you to be with HER. Poppy's doing the same thing. It's just a different HER. I swiped at the tears now streaming down my cheeks.

Mom's grip on my wrists tightened while she spoke urgently, "Andy, your grandfather loves Jane Ellen, and she him. They deserve some happiness together. Please don't ruin this for them."

I tore away from my mother, and the plate

slipped out of my hands. It tumbled to the floor and

shattered. The pieces gathered around our feet.

"But, what about me, Mom? What about if I'm

happy?" She bent to collect the broken shards as I

escaped to my bedroom, slamming the door closed

behind me.

Chapter 5

"You actually broke your mother's plate?

Uh-oh. I'd prob'ly be in really big trouble for that.

Were you?

"No, my mom didn't seem to care about that.

She was more concerned about what I had said before

I ran out of the room." I sat quietly, remembering,

while Lisa pushed gently against her loose tooth.

"Go on, Daddy. I want to hear more."

Saturday morning, Valentines Day, began

with a pelting snowfall, blowing through the streets

and clogging intersections. My best friend Leon

rode over on his bike in the snowy afternoon. We

had big plans for an overnight stay, he and I –

nachos and video games until Mom couldn't stand our noise any longer. I was especially glad to have Leon's company since the Three Musketeers were on the outs. The three of us – Mom, Poppy, and me – were barely speaking since last night's broken plate. Guess it was just hard to know what to say.

All morning Mom and Poppy had waited to hear from the dentist's office. Just as Leon arrived, Dr. Benton's office called. Mom answered the trilling phone. Yes, someone would pick up the partial before the five pm closing time. Poppy, nervous from the wait, put on his coat and grabbed his car keys. He lisped instructions to Mom about making sure his clothes were ready for the big date, then turned to me. "I need you boyth to ride along.

Your mother wantth thome thinth from the grothery for dinner. You can go there while I run netht door to the dentitht's offithe. Okay?"

I glanced at Leon, who was stifling a grin over Poppy's speech troubles. He sounded so funny with those teeth missing. Leon shrugged in agreement with my grandfather's request. "Sure, we can get the groceries. Just let me make a pit stop first," I answered Poppy. It was the first full sentence I had spoken to him all day. I dashed down the hallway toward the bathroom while Leon retrieved his coat from the floor of my room.

From the bathroom I could hear Mom and Poppy discussing details of the upcoming evening – a dance at the Senior Center, followed by the "big question", the proposal to Miss Jane over coffee at the shop. Poppy had shown us the ring earlier, a sparkly golden thing in a blue velvet box. He'd carried it around in his pocket for days. Their voices droned on, saying things I didn't really want to hear. Not that it mattered, I knew. Poppy had decided, and I would have to live with that.

I pushed on the toilet handle and watched absently as the water gurgled and swirled, rushing down, down, down. But, wait. The whole process was reversing. The toilet was instead refilling fast, much faster than a normal flush. It was rising up to the lower edge of the bowl. The water was lapping at the rim. It was OVERFLOWING!!! Gurgling up and out, over the side of the toilet bowl, lapping and running down onto the tiled floor, swirling across to the bath mat, and sending the wastebasket awash to the opposite wall. I just stood there, watching, fascinated for a few seconds, then realized what I hadn't done. I'd forgotten to jiggle the handle. I threw the door open and screamed into the hallway, "Mom, HELP. The toilet's overflowing!!

Everybody, Leon included, waded into the bathroom. Poppy grabbed up towels and began the major mop-up as Mom scrunched down over the gurgling commode to reach the shut-off valve. The water slowed and finally stopped. The toilet burped loudly and sighed, then stood quiet at last. Leon watched the whole incident, his mouth gaping wide in astonishment and teen-age glee. "Holy Pete," he kept repeating. We Three Musketeers, plus one, surveyed the damage—a floating roll of soggy toilet paper, the bath mat lying in a sodden heap below the window, and the tub filled with sopping towels. Poppy knelt in wet jeans, still mopping and wringing. "You didn't jiggle the handle, did you?" I made no answer.

"Claire, call Beggley Plumbing. Ron told me a couple of weekth ago that if thith happened again, he'd come as thoon as pothtible." Poppy continued to mop. "I'll thtay with it until he arriveth, explain wha'th going on. Andy, you'll have to go after my teeth yourthelf. Ride your bike. And, be back thoon. I'll thtill have time to get ready for the danthe."

Chapter 6

Mom handed me a short grocery list and a twenty-dollar bill. Since the grocery and the dentist's office shared the same shopping area, I could make short work of both stops, Mom said. We boys left in the afternoon snow and rode straight to Dr. Benton's office. Once away from the house, Leon hooted loudly about the overflowing toilet, laughing most of the way to Dr. Benton's door. "And, your grandfather," Leon bellowed as we pedaled toward town, "he spits everywhere!"

The box containing Poppy's upper plate sat on the counter in the waiting room. I explained why I was picking up the teeth rather than Poppy himself or my mother. There had been an 'emergency' at my house. "Yeah," Leon began loudly, "the toi. . . " I elbowed him in the ribs.

"Shut up, Leon," I hissed.

Stuffing the tooth box into my coat pocket, we left there and headed across the mall to Harper's Market. Leaning our bikes against a huge snow mound, the result of clearing the parking lot from earlier snowfalls, we trudged through the slush to the door. The door had just opened for us when Leon slapped my shoulder, "Look. There goes Jingles."

Leon didn't need to tell me that. I could hear the rhythmic chinketa-chinketa-chinketa sound long before I spotted the source. A huge mongrel dog went loping across the store lot. Dull brown fur, dirt-matted, hung clumped on legs and tail. One ear

stood at attention as the other lay limp and useless

across the dog's watery eyes. Several links of chain

on the dog's collar banged together as he ran,

making the chinketa-chinketa sound. Jingles was

his name because he did—jingle, that is. A town

stray, the mud-matted mongrel lived beneath the

front porch of the old deserted Garrett house on the

edge of town.

Old Carson Garrett, Jingles' last owner, had

tried unsuccessfully to keep the dog chained to his

front porch post. A nasty man who hated life in

general, and people in particular, Garrett treated

the dog very badly. So, Jingles often broke free,

running away to town in search of food, anything

that might serve as a next meal. When Garrett died,

Jingles simply went on scavenging for food in town

and sleeping under the sagging porch. Several

people had tried, and failed, to corral the animal.

Even the local Humane Society had all but given up

on ever snagging Jingles. The dog catchers had

sacrificed hats, gloves, jacket sleeves, and even a

finger or two to the cause. It had come down to

allowing Jingles to fend for himself through the

winter months, then make another attempt at

catching him once spring arrived.

Jingles had a split personality, kind of a cross

between Little Orphan Annie and Jabba the Hut.

The Annie side—mud covered and hungry eyed—

drew pity and an offered hand from folks ignorant

of Jingles' duel nature. Then Jabba the Hut—vicious, snarling—would spring violently to bite that offered hand. A true scavenger, he patrolled town streets regularly, taking for himself whatever hit the ground—hats, gloves, keys, wallets, women's scarves, homework assignments—anything that could be squirreled away under that old porch. Jingles ate from garbage cans and ran panting through neighborhoods, frightening women and children, a real embarrassment to the animal control officer.

We watched as Jingles shied away from an approaching car and skulked over to inspect a snow pile. Raising one leg to christen it in yellow, he trotted on around the parking lot. "Stupid thief,"

Leon wiped his runny nose on his red glove. "Mom made me chase that dumb dog around all one afternoon last week."

"Yeah? What'd he take this time?"

"My sister dropped her hat at the bus stop, and Mom was sure Jingles had swiped it. Begged me to look for it. My sister's gone through four hats already this winter. Can't hold on to nothin'."

"Any luck?" I asked.

"Nah. I guess he'd already taken it to his stash. There's no way I'm going to dig around under that filthy old porch," Leon snorted. "Hey, come on. Let's get those groceries. I'm starving."

We walked through the auto-door and saw Ginny Rae standing behind the register. Leon stopped dead, his jaw dropping in awe. The redhead Ginny was his latest love interest, and he stood, awestruck in her presence. I elbowed him hard through his coat and finally reached out to drag him down the nearest aisle. "Come on, Leon. You can ogle your sweetie later. We're in a hurry. Remember?"

"Yeah. Forgot about that." Leon shook himself back to consciousness and followed me through the grocery.

We finished our business at the market and mounted our bikes, ready to ride on home. Leon's mouth started running overtime about Ginny Rae while we rode together down the snowy street. I teased my buddy about her being an older woman.

After all, she was fifteen and a sophomore in high school. Both of us were lowly eighth-graders. Finally, Leon stopped chattering. We rode in silence for a few minutes. He chuckled then. "Hey, can I see those teeth, Andy?"

"What for?" His request confused me at first, until I remembered I was talking to crazy Leon.

"Let me try them on."

"Ewwwww. Somebody else's teeth in your mouth. You are sick, man. Besides, I'm not taking any chances. My grandfather would have a cow if anything happened to his partial plate today." I rode on past him, "I gotta' get it to him. Can you put on some speed?"

"Man, wait 'til the guys at school hear how you had Poppy's teeth in your pocket. That's a hoot. Maybe we should take a run down to Ben's house. He'd get a real laugh over them. Yeah, let's do that." Leon's excitement over such a joke made me a little ticked off.

"Aw Leon, let's just get back to my house. You said you were hungry. I am too."

"Come on, Andy. Can I at least see 'em. I've never had a good look at a partial plate before. Both my parents have their own teeth. They brush and they floss, brush and floss, brush and floss. And, they're always on my case about me taking care of my teeth. Did I brush today? Did I floss? Sometimes I just want to spit!" Leon hooted loudly, "Hey, that was a good one, huh. " He stopped his bike right in front of mine. "Just one look, Andy. Your grandpa won't ever even know."

"Alright." I halted beside him. "I'll let you look. Then, we're going home and you're going to shut up about these stupid teeth." I took off my glove and began to fish about in my pocket for the little box. Empty. My bike hit the ground while I dug in both pockets, then patted myself down like a policeman searching a criminal for some hidden weapon. Nothing. Leon and I stared at each other, open-mouthed, for long seconds. Leon grabbed the grocery sack and clawed through it. No little box.

"Holy Pete! What'd you do with it?"

"The grocery store . . . I must've pulled the box out when I brought the money out of my pocket. It has to be back at Harper's with the cashier." Jumping on my bike, I sped away back to the grocery. Leon followed. Charging through the door and right up to Ginny Rae's cash register, I fell across the conveyor. She stood chewing her gum wad and twisting her hair. "Ginny, did I leave a little white box here?"

She curled her lip at me and sighed in a very bored fashion. "No," was her simple answer.

"But, I'm sure I left it here. It fell out when I pulled that twenty dollar bill from my pocket," I pleaded with her.

"Just now when we got the cookies and hot dogs, and the nacho stuff," Leon added.

Again, Ginny Rae puffed a sigh, "No, it's not here."

"Please, can you look? Maybe somebody else . . . " Ginny's index finger tied a knot in her long red hair. "It was white. A little box about so big," I measured the air with finger and thumb.

"I said no!" Ginny's impatient voice barked. "There's no box here. Now move away from my register! I have customers to check out." She dismissed us with a frown and turned to the woman in line behind me. "Good afternoon, Mrs. Blaine. Did you find everything you needed?"

Slumping out of the store, we stood outside in the cold, trying to guess what had happened to Poppy's partial. Leon pointed to the mound of snow in the parking lot where we had rested our bikes before going into Harper's the first time. "Could you have dropped the box there when you pulled off your gloves and stuffed them in your pockets?" We raced to the snowpile, our breath fogging our faces.

The mound, once a hill of freshly moved snow, had become a sodden brown and muddy mess. Leaves and sticks, old candy wrappers, a discarded fast food bag or two were embedded in the snow mound. It was a huge repository of muddied snow and trash, and tracked all around were dog paw prints. Holes had been scratched in several spots. Jingles! My stomach took a leap, and I was nearly sick right there on the spot. I was sure of it. Jingles had the little white box. He had carried my grandfather's teeth away in his own mouth. Together Leon and I searched the parking lot for the mutt, straining to hear the familiar chinketa-chinketa of his chains. I caught sight of him loping away toward home, his home on the edge of town.

We followed him with our eyes. Leon just shook his head and reached for his bike. Me too. Jumping astride, we started toward the old deserted Garrett house, it's front porch a hiding place for countless lost items, including one little white box with Dr. Benton's office logo stamped across the top.

Chapter 7

"I don't think I'd like that old dog very much. He sounds mean."

"That's what we thought too, Lisa. All us kids in town stayed clear of him."

Her eyes were big and round with fear. "I just couldn't have followed him the way you and Leon did."

"We had no choice, sweetheart. I had to find those teeth."

"Tell me, Daddy. What happened next?" I helped her pop her head through the neck of her PJ shirt and continued the story.

We slid to a halt in the snow-covered yard. Jingles was there, his yellow eyes gleaming at us from under the porch. Leon and I stood together, trying to decide our next move. "I gotta' see if he has the box," I told Leon. Creeping in for a better look, I was greeted by a low-pitched rumble, a throaty growl from Jingles. He intended to protect what was his. I made a hasty retreat back to Leon's side.

He stood waiting, beating his hands together for warmth. "Is it there?" Did you see the box, Andy?"

"I can't tell. It's too dark, and Jingles sure doesn't want anyone near that porch," I mumbled. I returned the yellow-eyed stare of the dog hunched in his porch cave.

"What're you gonna' do?" Leon wheezed out. The cold air caught his words and amplified them loudly.

I flung my gloved hands wildly overhead. "I don't know yet! Let me think." Pacing in the snow, my mind worked for a plan, any plan. I thought aloud then. "I have to get that box. Mom will never believe that I just lost it. She's sure to think I did this on purpose. She knows how I hate losing Poppy to Miss Jane." I whipped around to face Leon and went on prattling into the air. "But, I would never pull such a stunt as this. I have to get those teeth. Leon, one of us has to keep that dog busy so that other can search under the porch. Any ideas?" I nearly begged.

"Keep THAT dog busy?" Leon motioned toward Jingles with a sharp head wag. "You can't be serious. You want to just chase him away from his territory? Oh sure. That's crazy, Andy. He'll take your leg off if you go anywhere near him. No way!"

I paced again. "There's gotta' be something we can do." I scuffed around in the snow for minutes while Leon followed me with suspicious eyes and bounced from left to right foot, then back again against the cold. Suddenly I grabbed at the grocery sack now lying on the ground beside our bikes and dumped the contents onto the ground at my feet. I kicked at the packaged foods. "This is how we get him."

"With that pile of stuff? Yeah I know he's a food hound, but there's not enough there to keep him occupied for long," Leon back away and made motions to pick up his bike.

"Think, Leon. Jingles' big goal in life is to eat. He'll go for all this stuff. The trick is to dole it out to him a little at a time . . . scatter it around the yard in small amounts. He'll be so busy chasing from pile to pile that he'll never notice someone digging around in his bed."

Leon listened with a disbelieving smirk on his face. "Andy, that will never happen. Listen, just let me ride back to town and find your Mom. I'll tell her what happened. Then she and Poppy can come get the box. I don't want to take on that big hairy animal. He nearly bit me last summer when I fought him over my baseball mitt. No way will I tangle with him again. No sir." Leon threw his leg across his bike now, ready to tear off out of the yard.

"Leon, I need your help. Remember who helped you cover up that little window accident at Mrs. Carter's last summer?" There. I had called in my big favor on him. I waited, arms folded across my chest and a superior look on my face. "You wouldn't want me to say anything to your mother about that, would you?"

Leon dropped the bike and marched toward me. "You wouldn't!"

"I'm begging you, Leon. This is a serious matter. I can't go back home without that box!"

"But, how long is that little amount gonna' last with such a big dog?"

"There's enough, I pressed my point. "Look . . . twelve hot dogs and eight buns, a big bag of chocolate chip cookies, the largest tortilla chip bag we could find, and nacho cheese dip." I held up the dip container, the one-pound size that Leon and I could easily work through in one night's stay. "It can be poured out on the ground in several places. He'll lap it up. And, the buns can be separated into the two halves. That makes sixteen bread parts. There's what, maybe four dozen cookies in this bag."

"SMALL cookies," Leon pointed out.

"Okay, they're small. But, if it's done right the stuff will stretch for several minutes' time. Keep him running from one spot to another in the yard. Busy enough not to notice someone crawling under the porch. I tell ya' it'll work." I stopped to survey Jingles still staring at us from under the porch. "It's just gotta' work."

"But, what if he doesn't like hot dogs. My sister throws up whenever . . .

"Leon, he's a dog. He'll eat anything remotely like food." I quickly gathered the groceries into my arms. "Now, are you gonna' continue this argument or help me get those teeth?" I was begging now. "Please Leon."

Chapter 8

With a huge groan Leon dropped his bike down in the snow. "Okay, okay. But, I don't handle Jingles. You keep him preoccupied while I search the porch."

"Great! Now just get close enough to see if the box is even under there. Don't try to go after it unless you can get your hands on it easily." I danced around Leon excitedly, jiggling the grocery sack in my hands. "Ready to give it a try?"

Leon drew in a hard breath. "Yeah, I guess so."

"First I gotta' open everything." I dumped the sack out at my feet and began tearing open the packages. When everything was open I turned and nodded at Leon. Then I moved slowly forward and waved my arms in Jingles' direction. "Hey Dog," I called out, "Come on out. I've got something for you. Are you hungry?"

"What a stupid question," Leon mumbled. He watched me drop the first hot dog close to the open side of the porch, the side where those yellow eyes gleamed. I could feel Jingles staring at me as I moved around the front of the house. I was sure his nose caught a big whiff of Oscar Mayer. I retreated a few steps to wait and listen. Chinketa-chinketa. Jingles was on the move, slowly belly-crawling out from his hiding place. He stayed on his belly, inching his way toward the hot dog, licking his chops with a long tongue. He snuffled at the hot dog, but pulled back a few inches, unsure of the situation. I

continued to stand and watch. Wait, wait. Jingles

slowly rose to his feet in slow motion, a hunter

stalking his prey. Suddenly, like a cobra striking, the

mutt reached and snatched the hot dog off the

ground. Gulp! It was down in one swallow.

I withdrew toward the side of the house and

away from the porch. Lifting a second hot dog in

the air, I waggled it back and forth, making sure

Jingles could see it in my hand. "Here you go, mutt.

I've got another treat. Come on now." Still backing

up, I dropped the treat in the snow. Jingles eyed me

suspiciously, but crept toward me and the hot dog.

"Leon," I hissed, "get going. Now's your chance. I've

got his attention for sure."

Leon bolted for the porch and hunched down to inspect Jingles' cluttered bed. "Peeeuuuuu, it stinks! Holy Pete, this is awful. There's dog doo and junk everywhere. This dog is a true kleptomaniac. There's some lady's scarf, and . . . hey, it's Jeff Peyton's history folder he lost last week. Man, he wouldn't want it back now. What a mess! Yeah, and there's an old wallet. It's all chewed up. Wonder if there's any money in it. Oh, I even see . . ."

I interrupted Leon's running list of lost items. "Never mind that other stuff. Do you see the tooth box?" I called out, still moving around the yard with that grungey animal jingling along behind, scarfing down hot dogs that I trailed before him in the snow.

"Hang on a minute. I'm still looking. It's pretty dark in here . . . hard to see." Leon was on his knees now, his head stuck into the porch opening. "Acccckkkkk," he gagged and coughed. Leon stood abruptly and stepped back from the porch. "That is so gross! Whey! Makes my eyes water. But, the box is there, Andy. I saw it over to the side, not so far in."

I threw the fourth hot dog down for Jingles . . . half of them were now in his belly. "That's great. Can you get it?"

"I don't know. Might not be able to reach it. Before that, though, I'll have to deal with the smell," Leon held his elbow across his nose.

"Try, Leon. Please try," I pleaded. "Use a stick or something to drag the box out."

Leon turned in a circle, searching the yard for anything that would extend his reach into the crawl space. "Nothing . . . I don't see anything to use," he moaned loudly.

My attention had turned away from Jingles, and the dog suddenly realized that Leon was very near his under-porch home. He bristled and growled. Bounding in Leon's direction, he'd nearly reached him when I threw a hot dog and actually hit Jingles in the head. He halted there and turned to devour the treat. Right away I lobbed another hot dog a few feet back my direction. "Come on back, mutt. I've got more for you." He again came my

way. "Go on, Leon. I've got him."

Leon, having run a few steps away from the

porch, now turned back. "Are you sure?"

"Yes, I'm sure. Listen, we don't have time to

search for a stick. Just get in there and find that

box!" Another hot dog landed in the snow.

"My Mom's gonna' kill me if I rip up one

more pair of jeans or get 'em all stained. And, what

about my coat? I'm dead for sure if I crawl around in

there with my coat on."

"Then take it off," I shouted loudly, too

loudly. Jingles shied away from me. I darted

forward, this time holding a hot dog out to him. I

wiggled it right before the dog's face while I sweet-talked, "Come on, buddy. Have another." Dropping it on the ground, I backed away as the eager Jingles grabbed it. He eyed me cautiously, all the while salivating and swallowing hurriedly.

"Leon, I'll give you every pair of jeans in my closet, even my new winter coat. Just get the box."

Jingles edged dangerously close while my guard was down. He snapped at my hand, the one that smelled of Oscar Mayer. I jumped away and sprinted to the opposite side of the yard. I shouted back at Leon, "He just got the last of the hot dogs. I'm starting on the cookies now. There's not much time left. Hurry!" I stuffed my hand into the bag and brought up several cookies. "Let's hope you like chocolate chips, dog." Then I worked myself around the beast and away from the fence that closed in the yard behind me. I wanted an escape route to my bike.

"Okay, okay." Leon scuffed back to the porch, dropped to his knees and disappeared under the old wooden structure. He mumbled and thumped about . . . and gagged once or twice, while I worked to keep Jingles occupied.

The dog eagerly trotted around the yard behind me now, his collar jewelry announcing each step. "Apparently you really like chocolate chips . . . maybe better than hot dogs." I hopped ahead of him, scattering a few cookies as I moved.

The dog's behavior was changing, and that scared me. He had dropped any pretense of fear, turning into a wiggling fur bag, licking his lips as he searched for the next treat. The cookies had won his heart and his confidence. They were disappearing into his toothy mouth too quickly, and I wondered if the nacho cheese sauce would hold his attention as easily as the cookies. "Leon, hurry, will ya'? He's going through this stuff really fast. I'm running out of goodies," I urged. "Any luck?"

"I think so," Leon grunted. "Yeah, yeah. Got it." More grunts sounded from under the porch as Leon pushed his way back into the fading winter sunlight .

I waited, still wary of Jingles' every move. I laid out a big pile of cookies and backed off. The mutt was still several feet to my right, licking his chops from the last cookie pile he'd just devoured. I

saw Leon's feet flailing around as he worked himself

out from under the porch. His booted feet kicked

and dug at the hard ground. Finally Leon stood up

and reached one filthy arm out to me. In his hand

lay the box, slightly misshapen and dirty brown

from its time in Jingles' secret stash.

Chapter 9

I was so relieved to see that tooth box! Forgetting the hungry dog, I started to move in Leon's direction when . . . THUD. Jingles rushed me, knocking me straight onto my face. I sputtered snow out of my mouth while Jingles danced on my back and chased around over my head. He whined and barked, the dog collar and chains jangling noisily. Lifting wet cheeks from the ground, I came away with snow crusted on my eyelids and nose. I spit away more dirty snow, raised up from my chest . . .and came eyeball to yellow eyeball with Jingles. He stared back and slowly curled his lips away from his teeth. This close, I saw the mud-caked muzzle, and I gasped from his dog breath, smelling of Oscar

Mayers and chocolate.

I froze in place. Jingles seemed frozen too,

except for the quivering lips. Both of us were

waiting to see who would make the first move.

Kinda' like a high noon gunfight, and I did not want

to draw down on this hothead. From my place on

the ground I called to Leon. "He's got me down. Get

back."

Leon was silent. For seconds I neither heard

nor saw anything other than Jingles' breathing and

that mouthful of teeth still showing on the dog's

face. Then a pair of muddy boots came into view as

Leon stepped closer to the pair of us, dog and boy in

the snow. "I'll get his attention. While he's looking

at me you get outta' there, Andy. But, don't make any fast moves! Slow and easy."

He shuffled toward us, calling sweetly to Jingles, "Here boy. Come on over here." He stooped and picked up a few cookie remnants that Jingles had missed. Holding them toward the dog, Leon crept closer. It worked. Jingles turned his attention to Leon just long enough for me to get off the ground and grab hold of the smashed grocery sack. I had fallen on it when I went down. I fished out the nacho dip. The container was bent open with some of the cheesy stuff loose in the plastic bag. I poured the remaining contents in a golden puddle on the snow. "Hey Jingles," I roughly called, "come and get it."

Jingles turned his huge head my way. He stood, deciding his next move. Then, staring back at Leon, Jingles moved his backside around in a half circle, wanting to inspect the cheese puddle. Finally he backed toward the cheese, and Leon saw his chance to escape to his own bicycle. For my part, I lobbed the dip container across the yard. With the grocery sack still dangling from my hand, I also grabbed my bike and joined Leon across the road.

I held out a hand. "Give it here." Leon produced the scruffy little box, wet and mud-caked. I took it, held it as if it were a magical thing, then stuffed it deeply into my coat pocket. "Thanks Leon. You're a good friend." I surveyed him closely.

"Wow. You're a real mess. And, you stink too. You really stink!"

"What'd I tell you about that dog's bed?" Leon leveled his eyes on me. "You owe me, Andrew Tate. You owe me big time," he grumbled with a half-smile as he threw one leg over his bicycle.

We both watched a few seconds more as Jingles, whining in anticipation, ran from spot to spot in the yard seeking more goodies. He found the empty dip container and busied himself with it as we rode away toward town.

"Boy, Leon was a reeeeaaallly good friend. I don't know if any of my friends would help me like that."

"That's true, Lisa. He's still a great friend. You remember Leon, don't you? We've spent time with him and his family at the lake. "

"Oh yeah. Now I do. He's the guy who acts so silly when he sings and plays his guitar."

I chuckled, "Yep, he's the one. Doesn't sing too well, does he?"

"Nope," Lisa agreed. "But, he's sure funny. Go on, Daddy. What happened next?"

Relieved that our ordeal was ended, and tired from effort and fright, we pushed toward home. I had gone only a few yards when Leon called over his shoulder, "Hey, what's for dinner? Jingles just ate it all, didn't he?"

"Maybe we can order pizza. They'll deliver, you know." I laughed. It felt great to have that little box tucked away in my pocket again. Leon broke into song . . . the pizza delivery tune from television. Pepperoni and an icy Coke was Leon's answer to a troubled spirit and weary body.

Suddenly, from behind us, a chinketa-chinketa sounded loudly, and a muddied fur mat with teeth caught at my pants leg. Jingles was there, gnashing and ripping madly. The dog ran between us, turning first to Leon's boot then back to mine, biting at the laces and leather. He did little harm, but the weight of his lunges kept throwing us off balance. We rode drunkenly along in the circus of bicycles and dog nipping at the pedals, until I remembered the hot dog buns and chips still swinging crazily in the grocery sack hanging from my handlebars.

Balancing single-handed, I dug in the bag for the buns. Ripping them open with my teeth, I flung the entire number of them in the air. We rode through a bread shower while Jingles slowed and stopped at the first bun to hit the pavement. He sniffed at it, then began to chomp away. Gulp, gulp, gulp. He mangled It between his teeth in record time. Galloping down the road toward the next bun, and us, he repeated the process. Sniff and snarf.

The chinketa-chinketa sounded in our ears as we continued to pedal madly, trying to put greater distance between us and the old brown mutt. I dared to peer over my shoulder. The buns were all gone! He was chasing us fiercely again, coming on swiftly, those heavy paws pounding the roadway. He got ever closer and I could hear his breath huffing in that barrel chest. Up ahead, Leon leaned into his work, pumping hard. He took off away from me as Jingles closed the distance between us.

One thing was left—the bag of tortilla chips. I gripped the bag between my teeth and pulled hard. The wind made by my own bike-riding caught the chips, scattering them in a wide arc. Jingles' steps slowed and he jangled from one chip pile to the next, crunching and chomping as he moved. I glanced back to see the dog enjoying his feast, then forced my tired legs to work even harder.

Speeding down the road, I spied Leon far ahead, waiting for me to catch up. He had slowed considerably. Relief spread through me, and I allowed myself to think about being home soon. But, like a recurring nightmare, Jingles was again at my heels—chinketa-chinketa. He grabbed my ankle in those strong jaws and jerked with his entire body. I struggled to regain my balance, but he persisted, throwing his whole dog self into the task of dismounting me. Suddenly the bike shot sideways right into a huge pine tree that stood at the road's edge. It connected with the tree, and I took flight up and over the handlebars, banged my head against the rough trunk, and slumped in a heap on the snow

carpet below the pine boughs.

Leon had halted several yards ahead and

saw the whole sickening incident. He sped back to

me and dropped to his knees on the whitened

ground beside me. "Holy Pete, Andy. You're

bleedin', man." He wiped a trickle of blood from my

forehead. "I'll get help. Just stay right here. Don't

get up!" Leon jumped astride his bike and rushed

toward town, leaving me alone in the cold on a

darkening road.

Chapter 10

My head hurt! I was miserable, wet and cold, as a terrific headache throbbed and thumped as I tried to move around. Besides that, there was Jingles. He had taken a stance just a few feet out from where I had landed. Those two golden eyes took in every move I made, and ears perked slightly with each of my groans. I eyed him warily, trying to decide a way to defend myself if need be.

I tried to stand against the pine tree, but my legs simply wouldn't hold me. I wobbled and slipped against the rough bark. Slumping back onto the ground, I glared at Jingles and uttered a weak command. "Go away, dog. Leave me alone."

He responded by edging two or three steps closer. Lowering his muzzle, Jingles sniffed the red-brown stain of my blood on the snow. I began to accept my inevitable fate . . . the dog was about to rip me up, leaving even more blood stain on the snow. I decided to close my eyes and wait, just wait.

It was coming, of that I was sure. Even with the headache drum-drum-drumming in my ears, my senses were afire. I felt Jingles move closer, yet closer. I heard his chest movements, smelled his hot dog-and cookie breath. I finally cracked one eye open to check the dog's position. He stood so very near, gazing at my forehead, the place from where blood slowly oozed across my nose and cheek. Jingles dropped to his belly and dragged himself forward. He began to whine, a moany whimpering sound that echoed in the woods behind us. Before I realized it, Jingles' raggedy old head was resting in my lap. He continued that ear-piercing whine, all the while rooting in my lap for my hand, not to bite, but to rest on his big head. I couldn't believe it. The dog actually wanted me to touch him, to pet him.

"Get away," I grumbled. I tried to push against his big body. The effort made my head pound even harder. I tried wiggling away from Jingles, but he kept up with me, staying in my lap. I shoved and pushed and pried, but no, Jingles wouldn't have it. He was on my lap to stay, whimpering softly and nuzzling his dirty brown muzzle under my gloved hands. Finally I gave in and gingerly touch the furry head, stroking lightly. Then I scratched his ears, and even spoke to him in soft tones. "It's okay, Jingles. I'm alright. Help will be here soon." While I talked the old dog relaxed more on my legs. He cuddled into me, and together we waited, warming each other in the darkening winter air.

"WOW!" Lisa exclaimed from beneath her covers. She'd climbed into bed as I'd continued with my story. Her little eyes drooped occasionally, but she worked to listen, to stay awake until the story's end. "Jingles turned out lots different than I thought he was. That must have been a real surprise, huh Daddy.

I guess sometimes things can really be different than they seem."

"That's so right, Lisa. You can always be surprised with how things turn out." I brushed her hair from her forehead. "Are you ready for sleep? It's awfully late, you know."

"No Daddy, please tell me more. I want to know what happens next. Does Leon come back for you?"

"Okay, Lisa. I'll finish my story. Now, where was I?"

"You were at the part where Jingles is sitting on . . . "she stopped to yawn widely. "Ooooo," Lisa suddenly cried.

"What is it, honey?"

Lisa's mouth formed a wide smile. She held up her open hand. There lay her front baby tooth, a glistening white nub. "Look, Daddy. My tooth came out." She stared at it in wonder. "It didn't even hurt."

"That's great, sweetheart. Here, let's tuck it under your pillow. The Tooth Fairy is sure to come before you wake in the morning and give you four quarters just like your brother got under his pillow."

"Do you think?" She turned back and grabbed the pillow's corner. Lisa slipped her little hand under, then patted the pillow twice and plopped her head back down. "Now," she rearranged her covers. "Go on with the story, please."

"Okay, but I need to finish fast. Your mother will be unhappy with both of is if you're not asleep very soon."

Chapter 11

The snow's white gave way to the hospital's white. I woke up in the emergency room, my head bandaged, Mom and Leon standing at my side. "How did I get here?" I mumbled to them. But, I already knew the answer even as I asked the question.

It hadn't taken long for the EMT's to arrive, and Jingles had waited with me, a faithful companion. The doctor had stitched up my forehead cut and gave Mom a good word on my x-rays. I did feel a little dizzy, however, so I simply listened while Leon related the story of our wild adventure.

When he finished, Mom shook her head in astonishment. "That's some tale, Leon. No wonder you were so stinky and filthy," she waved a hand before her nose. "Your mother will be very glad to see that you're in clean hospital scrubs while those clothes are tied in a garbage bag. I called to tell her that I'll bring you home, safe and sound."

"Thanks Mrs. Tate. But, I'm still worried she'll freak out over my winter coat. She'll probably just want to throw it away."

"She'll definitely want to throw it away. I'm sure of that." Mom chuckled softly. "Don't worry, Leon. I think we can manage to find another coat for you. That's more than fair payment for the help you gave Andy in this little adventure." Then, turning back to me, Mom continued, "I'm so glad you weren't hurt more severely, Andy. "That old dog could have . . . her voice trailed off as she fingered my hair.

I reached up to gingerly touch my bandaged forehead. "Mom, about Jingles. He acted so funny after I hit the tree. He whined and whimpered, even laid down across my legs and kept me warm. It was so weird."

"Yes, the EMT crew told me about the dog lying in your lap when they arrived on the scene. He wouldn't let them near you for several minutes, then barked and growled while they took care of you -- stood guard, and even tried to climb into the ambulance after they loaded your gurney inside. That doesn't fit my mental picture of Jingles."

"I know. It's like he knew I was hurt. Soon after Jingles crawled into my lap I stopped shivering, from both the cold and fear." I stopped momentarily. "And, you know what happened next?" Both Mom and Leon looked at me expectantly. "That dirty old mutt fell asleep in my arms." I shook my bandaged head slowly in disbelief. "I guess that's when I fell asleep too."

"Unreal," Leon sighed.

"Unexpected, I'd say. Sometimes we get surprises in life, from dogs and people." Mom pursed her lips, then turned to pick up the glass of ice water by my bed. "Here, take a drink. The doctor says to keep up the fluids, Andy."

"Yeah, I bet Jingles just liked the smell of your gloves. Oscar Mayer, you know." My friend poked my arm.

"Ouch!" I yelped. "Watch it, Leon. Everything hurts, you know."

"Oops. Sorry."

I saw the little dirty-white tooth box lying on my bed tray and reached out to pick it up. Fingering it lightly, I questioned Mom, "Is Poppy coming?"

"He called to say he's on his way now. The plumber finished just minutes after I called to tell him about your accident." Then Mom addressed

Leon. "I can drop you off before going on home with my patient. I told your mother I'd do that."

"But Mom, Leon was going to spend the night. Can he still stay? Please?"

She cocked her head and waved a finger at me. "Andrew, you're going to need your . . . "

"Mom, I'm alright. My headache is gone. I've got this great white turban, and the doctor said I'm good to go. You heard him."

"Oh, I don't know son. I think maybe . . . " She stopped to survey both our disappointed faces. "Well, I guess it will be alright. But, you have to take it easy. No running around. Your backside firmly planted on the couch. When I say 'bedtime' no arguments. Do you understand?"

"We understand," Leon and I answered in chorus. We smiled broadly at each other and did a gentle high-five. Then I remembered. "There is one problem, Mom. We don't have anything for dinner."

"I take it that Jingles ate everything?"

"Yep," Leon answered. "That, or else anything left is scattered along the road."

"Well, I suppose we could order in a pizza. That delivery place is running a special on heart-shaped pepperonis in honor of Valentines Day."

"Valentines Day. That's today . . . " My eyes widened as I remembered. "Oh Mom, Poppy and Miss Jane . . . "

The curtain on my ER cubicle flew back with

a mighty shove and Poppy stomped to my beside. He was huffing and puffing from hurrying across the outside parking lot. Mom urged him to relax and sit down on the edge of the gurney. "Nonthenthe. I'm fine, jutht fine. How'th the boy?"

His big hands wandered down both my arms and he gently reached two fingers to the turban bandage I wore. "Are you alright, Andy?" He lifted my chin to inspect my face closely. "Thon, that phone call from your mother really thcared me." Tapping my cheek, Poppy grinned and snorted. "But, I can thee that thingth will be fine with you in no time. What happened? Jutht the thort verthion, pleathe."

Leon wound up for his explanation of the

day's wildness over Jingles and the pine tree, but Mom intervened with her own telling. Poppy smiled at the idea of hot dogs and cookies and tortilla chips scattered on the roadway. Then he noticed Leon's clothing. "Are you on thtaff at the hothpital now?" he asked him.

"What?" Leon's confused voice asked. "Oh, they gave me these scrubs to wear since my stuff was so filthy. They're in this garbage bag. See?"

Poppy glanced into the bag that Leon held open for him. "Wow! That'th rank, boy. Clothe it up! Wait, what'th that?" Poppy reached into the bag with thumb and index finger. He held up a grimey piece of pink knitwear.

"Oh yeah. I forgot about it in all the excitement over Andy's accident. I found my kid sister's hat under Jingles' porch." He grabbed the hat from Poppy and stuffed it back into the garbagebag. "Mom's gonna' be so happy I found it." He beamed at us.

"Not so much, Leon. Not so much." Mom chuckled.

Just then the ER nurse arrived with discharge papers. We were gathering things to leave the hospital when Poppy suddenly spoke. "My teeth. What about my teeth?"

"They're right here, Poppy." I proudly handed the small box to him. He scrubbed at the dirt smearing Dr. Benton's logo, then opened the lid. There, between cotton batting lay his partial plate. Two brand new front teeth, exact images of the former ones, were in place. He picked up the piece to inspect it more closely. Then, he replaced the lid on the box and turned to me and Leon.

"I want to thank you boyth for what you did. You were very brave, both of you. I'm tho happy to have my thmile back."

"Well, I shouldn't have lost the box in the first place." I hung my head.

"No, I thouldn't have put that bubble gum in my mouth in the firtht plathe. That'th the truth of it." Poppy declared.

"Okay, so everything has ended well." Mom bustled around the little cubicle again, gathering things. "Let's get out of here."

"I'm ready." I started to climb from the gurney.

"Thlow down, Andy. Let me get the car and bring it up to the ER door outthide firtht," Poppy interrupted me.

"But, you have plans. You can't go with us," I reminded him.

"I do?" Poppy seemed confused.

"Yes," I answered him. "It's Valentines Day. I seem to remember that you have a date."

"It ith? I do?" Poppy's words stumbled out.

"Now, get out of here. You can pick up some flowers for Miss Jane at the hospital gift shop. They're still open." Mom pushed him toward the hallway.

He gave us a bewildered look, then smiled and nodded. Poppy turned and walked past the curtain, then stuck his head back inside. "Wait here for a few minuteth longer, everybody. I'll be right back."

I dropped back onto the gurney, giving Mom a questioning eye. Leon twitched his face, then turned back to us. We waited just seconds before Poppy bounded back to my cubicle, his mouth tightly closed. Suddenly he took a stage bow and laid both hands, laced together, below his chin.

Elbows flying out and up, Poppy opened his mouth into a wide grin. "How do I look?" he asked the three of us.

We burst into laughter. "You look great, Dad!"

"But, how do you sound?" Leon asked the important question.

Poppy took a deep breath and recited, "Sally sells sea shells by the seashore!"

We applauded and cat-called our approval. He bowed low and swept his baseball cap through the air. Our good-byes accompanied his exit.

Chapter 12

Finally Mom, Leon, and I were on our way too. She left Leon with me and brought the car to the ER exit door. The nurse wheeled my chair out the door and Leon stuffed himself and the smelly garbage sack into the back of our SUV. Mom helped me climb into the front seat. We belted ourselves in. Leon then wanted to know if the pizza we ordered had to be heart-shaped. Mom just shook her head and smiled at him from the rearview mirror.

"Mom, how soon before Poppy and Miss Jane will be married?"

"Soon, I would guess. Does it matter to you?" her voice showed concern.

"Well, my birthday is coming in a couple months. Do you think they'd choose have their wedding on my birthday?"

"Andy, if you don't want to share . . . "

"Hey, I'd like it if they chose that day."

You would?" Surprised, Mom asked why.

"I could remember their anniversary more easily that way. I don't want to miss a single one of them."

Mom reached out for my hand. She smiled, a smile that went all the way to her eyes. She shook her head then, and laughed aloud.

"What's so funny, Mrs. T?" Leon asked.

Oh, it's my Dad and those teeth."

Both of us waited to hear her finish her thought. "He makes me think of Mount Rushmore."

Lisa yawned widely and smiled then, the new gap in her teeth showing. "Was Miss Jane a pretty bride, Daddy? Mommy always says that at weddings – a pretty bride. Was she?"

"Oh yeah. She was a very pretty bride." I smiled too, remembering.

"That's a great story, Daddy. I think I'll ask for that one again."

I reached to tuck the blanket under her chin. "I'll tell it again, but I need to break it into two or three bedtimes. It's way too long

for one night." I patted her knee. "Well,

goodnight, little lady. Sleep tight." I turned to

the doorway, but her voice called me back.

"Wait, Daddy. What happened to

Jingles?"

"Jingles? That scruffy old dog that you

thought was so mean and scary?"

"But, he turned out to be not so bad,

didn't he? He kept you warm, Daddy, there in

the snow under the pine tree. What happened

to him?" She was suddenly wide awake,

sitting up and clasping her arms around her

knees.

"Well, two days later, after my run-in with the pine tree, a lady member of the EMT crew who had helped me drove her own pickup out to the Garrett house. She and her husband managed to lure Jingles into the truck's camper shell. They took that ugly animal to the vet's office, and first he got a bath."

"I bet," Lisa giggled. "What next? Wait, did Jingles try to bite anyone?"

"Not at all. He turned out to be a real sweet guy. The lady and her husband took Jingles to their home, where he lived with the family and their other pets for a long time."

Lisa smiled and let her head drop back to the pillow. "I really like that part of your story, Daddy."

"And, guess how the lady EMT coaxed Jingles into the back of her pickup truck," I laughed. "She used a package of Oscar-Mayer hot dogs." We laughed together as Lisa rolled side to side on her bed, her whole little body shaking with happiness.

"Now, you HAVE to get to sleep." I reached down to pull the blanket around her shoulders. Surprisingly, Lisa settled down immediately. Her face stretched in yet another big yawn.

As I turned away, her sleepy voice

followed, "Daddy, my other front tooth will

come out too, won't it? To make room for

another permamunt?"

"Yes, it will."

"Good." She curled onto her side and

settled in for the night.

I wondered aloud, "Why is that good,

Sweetheart?"

She mumbled sleepily into her pillow.

"Because when it comes out I'll talk like Poppy. My

ethes' will thound funny." I laughed and wished her a

good night's sleep. "Thee you in the morning," Lisa's

sleep voice teased. Then, "And, one more thing,

Daddy. When both my permamumts come back in I'll

look like that guy on Mount Rushmush."

I chuckled, "Yeah, that's true. Flipping off the

light, I looked down on my daughter just in time to

see her slip her hand under the bed pillow. She felt

around for her stored tooth, then smiled sleepily and

snuggled into the blanket. I stood a bit longer,

watching my daughter drift off to sleep.

Made in the USA
Middletown, DE
15 June 2015